Climbing an Unnamed Mountain

Climbing an Unnamed Mountain

Poems by

Michael Walls

© 2022 Michael Walls. All rights reserved.
This material may not be reproduced in any form, published,
reprinted, recorded, performed, broadcast,
rewritten or redistributed without
the explicit permission of Michael Walls.
All such actions are strictly prohibited by law.

Cover design by Shay Culligan

ISBN: 978-1-63980-149-7

Kelsay Books
502 South 1040 East, A-119
American Fork, Utah 84003
Kelsaybooks.com

For my mother, Juana Fae Westmoreland Walls
1924–1985

and

the Marshallese people who have suffered
and will continue to suffer because of actions by my country

Acknowledgments

My heartfelt gratitude to Karen Kelsay for believing in and publishing this book and to all the others who helped make this collection possible: Amy Pence for encouraging me to begin and then keep writing poems about Bikini Atoll and for being first reader for many of those poems; Cathy Carlisi, Beth Gylys, Amy Pence, Jennifer Wheelock and Ashley Grice from my writing group who provided insightful critiquing for several of these poems via zoom during the pandemic; Mary Ricketson for being first reader for some of these poems and for critiquing them during poem swaps; Luke Hankins who helped with final edits and proofreading; the editors who first published some of these poems; and last, but far from least, the women from She's Wired who came to my rescue and helped me save all of my poems including the final edited manuscript of this book when my computer was crashing. Thank you all.

Grateful appreciation to editors of the following journals where some of these poems first appeared, sometimes in slightly different forms or with different titles.

Bryant Literary Journal: "Chicago—1965"

Brooklyn Review: "The Day a Love Affair Ended"

The Cape Rock: "Write-Off," "Bombs and Billy Graham"

DASH: "Operation Crossroad," "Juana," "The Last Remaining Eden"

Evening Street Review: "A Ten - Dollar Bill," "Castle Bravo"

Golden Poetry: "Naked"

the Kerf: "Kayaking the Rio Grande,"
  "Bikini Atoll"

The Main Street Rag: "Climbing an Unnamed
  Mountain"

New Zoo Poetry Review: "Rainbow Connection"

Red Rock Review: "Birthday #76"

San Pedro River Review: "Breath"

South Florida Poetry Journal: "Erythromelalgia,"
  "Baking Banana Bread"

Steam Ticket: "Rushing Down 57th Street,"
  "We See Them for Years"

An earlier version of the poem, "Naked," appeared in the chapbook *The Blues Singer,* authored by Michael Walls and published by The Frank Cat Press, 2003.

The epigraph for Part Two is from the song "Diamonds and Dust," written and sung by Joan Baez, published in 1975, used with permission from copyright © Chandon Music.

Contents

Part One

Climbing an Unnamed Mountain	15
Chicago – 1966	16
Juana	17
Write-Offs	19
We See Them for Years	20
Saturday Farmer's Market,	
Four Days Before Christmas	22
Grass Wars	23
Bombs and Billy Graham	25
4:00 A.M.	27
Rainbow Connection	28
Kayaking the Rio Grande	29
Houses	30
Trees	31
Breath	32
Brotherhood	33
That Day – Sandy	34
End of Summer	36

Part Two

Howdy	39
Erythromelalgia	40
Earth Day – 2020	42
A Ten - Dollar Bill	43
Rushing Down Fifty-Seventh Street	44
The Day a Love Affair Ended	45
Naked	46
Sunrise	47
Birthday #76	48

Part Three

Broken Promises	51
Bikini Atoll	53
Jolet Jen Anij	54
One Sunday – After Church, February 1946	57
Operation Crossroads – July 1, 1946, First Nuclear Bomb Test at Bikini	61
Castle Bravo – March 1, 1954, World's First Thermo-Nuclear Bomb Test	62
One Day in August – 1960	64
The Last Remaining Eden *	65
King Tides	66
Pantoum for Junior	67
Island Boy	69

Part Four

In America – November 2016	73
In Szentendre	74
Charlottesville	76
Miquel	77
Two Little Girls	78
The News	79
The End	82
Baking Banana Bread	83

Part One

It's your road, and yours alone, others may walk it with you, but no one can walk it for you.
—Rumi

Climbing an Unnamed Mountain

The trail crosses a road where daffodils
shiver in eerie cold toward the end
of this longest winter, passes through
a pine grove, planted by some long-gone
homesteader, crosses a drought-starved
creek that marks the edge of the valley.
From here, the path begins its climb,
switching its way through soundless winter
woods—naked March oaks and poplars—
into dark coves carved by eons
of moving water, then back into the sun
where it looks down on a pasture, cut
by the rut of a creek that grows smaller
at every turn. At the last switch-back,
the silence is broken by groans—
a fallen tree, wedged, rubbing between
two trunks—crying out the birth of spring.
At the summit, a treeless patch of granite
slabs, held together by out-of-sync wild
flowers and last year's grass. A clock-
confused robin crouches out of the wind
behind a lone beetle-battered pine.

Chicago – 1966

I remember you well. Sidewalks were slush,
snow piled along the edges. We were young.
We met the night I first heard "Nowhere Man."
When "Zorba the Greek" played on the juke box,
you grabbed my hand, tried to teach me
a traditional Greek dance. We walked down
to Rush Street, then you took me home—
tentative crunches up steps, gritty with salt,
that led to your front door. We sat on your floor
and talked. I watched how you twisted your hair
into coils that hung a few seconds, then fell
to your shoulders, felt tendons on your neck,
tight as E strings, while you told me about
a boyfriend, sent to Viet Nam, who came home
and beat you up. Later—tenderness, kisses,
caresses came with the wine. In the morning
your hand shook as you poured the coffee, told
me I couldn't see you again. Your boyfriend
was getting out of the army and coming home.

Juana

for my mother, Juana Fae Westmoreland Walls
(1924—1985)

I dozed. I woke and stared until I could
make out the rise and fall of the covers.
Over and over that last night, I went
to your bedside, rubbed my finger
through the stubble of your hair, across
creases flattening into lines like clouds
fading, sliding from your face.

I was five, house steeped in smells
of Sunday dinner. We lay on a big
double bed. I whined that I was
too big for a nap. Yapping dogs,
screams of older cousins playing
in the yard drifted through
the open window while you read
me the funny pages and re-told me
a story, told to you by your mother
when you were my age, while the two
of you sat together beneath the same
gnarled blackjack oak in the clearing
by the creek where you and I went
to practice spelling. I laid my head
against your stomach and fell asleep.

You were a young mother. Your hair
was pretty and long. Depending
on the sun, it was strawberry or
the color of just-cut hay. Later,
you wore it short. Hairdresser's tint
darkened it to a deeper red each year.

When it returned after the chemo
—a blond-gray blend, lighter than
when you were young—I wanted
to see it grow long again. The wig
you wore in your coffin was red.

Write-Offs

I place them in brown paper bags:
a T-shirt, once stuck to my back
by marathon sweat while I shivered
on the corner of 74th Street
and Central Park West, when Erin
was late to meet me at the finish line,
wool socks that wicked away water,
kept my feet from getting blisters
when I slipped on slick rocks crossing
swollen creeks, a belt I quit wearing
when the friend who gave it to me
stopped being my friend, a tie I once
chose to impress a jury, then shuffled
out of the rotation like an ace pitcher
who lost his fastball, a towel that hung
on the oven door, mingling pungent
aromas of onions and garlic with spilt
milk's sour sweetness while keeping
my hands dry, sheets my fevered body
lay between the day I couldn't get out
of bed—all pieces of my life.

Tomorrow, I'll take them to a homeless
shelter. The attendant will ask me
if I want a receipt for tax purposes.

We See Them for Years

*Blessed be ye poor: for yours
is the kingdom of heaven.*

*Blessed are ye that hunger now:
for ye shall be filled.*
                         Luke 6:20—21

Then one day they disappear.

I

He was a fixture on the corner
of Moreland and Ponce de Leon,
first selling *The Great Speckled Bird,*
later pulp mags—same black tank-top,
same long hair, once blond, then gray.
Everybody knew him as Wolf. A story
in *Creative Loafing* after he died, said
his name was Wilton Hugh Thomas.

II

She sat on a wall near the courthouse,
each time, frailer than before.
If I wasn't running late and no cop
in sight, I'd cross the street, slip
her some money. She'd say,
God bless you sir. I'd say, *hope
it helps.* One day, coming down
the courthouse steps, I looked
over her way, but she wasn't there.
Only then did I realized I had not
seen her in months.

III

No matter the weather or the month
—trench coat hanging off his shoulders
like a tent—he walked up and down
Ponce de Leon and North Highland.
It must be thirty years since I last saw
him. It was a slow Sunday afternoon
at American Roadhouse. He slipped
in while the wait-staff leaned against
the wall between the bathrooms
and the kitchen talking about high
rent, bad dates and the brunch crowd
sauntered out. He settled into a booth
—a mass of earth tones against red
vinyl—ordered fried chicken, mashed
potatoes and chocolate ice cream.
When the check came, he counted
out coins, dropped them—a few
at a time—into the waiter's palm,
then sat with his water. After a few
minutes, he reached beneath his coat,
retrieved more coins, stacked them
carefully beside his glass.

Saturday Farmer's Market, Four Days Before Christmas

Like a piece of urban art, a person
wrapped in a blanket showing only
sockless ankles and eyes, sits
on a bench at the hill's crest,
where cold wind whips hardest.

Shoppers hurry past—from parking
lot to tents arrayed with vegetables,
flowers, bread and honey—then run
back to the parking lot. She/he says
nothing. Nobody stops. My bare

hands like ice cubes, I rush
to the bakery that sells French
bread, grab a "Provincial Herb
Omelet in a Baguette," hurry
back to the car and home.

Settled in my favorite chair, cup
of fresh brewed cinnamon coffee,
carols on the radio, presents
wrapped in pretty paper beneath
a tinseled fir tree, I remember
the strange person at the market.
Nobody stopped.

Grass Wars

My father liked to plant grass:
the yard surrounding our house,
quilt-like patches in nearby woods,
ground reclaimed from beneath
a worn-out barn, the vacant lot
across the one-lane dirt road.

In summer, the supper table
became a war zone, each of us
intent on protecting our turf.
The minute I was told to *cut
the grass,* tempers flared. Battle
lines were drawn. In the fights
that followed I honed backtalk
and arguing skills for upcoming
duels—rebellious son with ideas
and old-school father locked
in a war over petty grievances—
substitutes for larger ones not
understood or resolved for years.

On a hot summer afternoon, decades
after our final truce, all of us kids
sat around him at the kitchen table
while he wrote checks to pay his bills.
When the last check was written,
he balanced his checkbook, laid it
on the table with a list of doctor's
and hospital bills, expected funeral
expenses and insurance information.

Outside, grass was turning sallow
and brittle while rain refused to fall.
*About my grave, I want it covered
with gravel. You kids shouldn't have
to worry about keeping it mowed.*

Bombs and Billy Graham

—February 21, 2018

Hemmed in, stalled by a line
of orange cones on I-75 / I-85
Connector, I hear Billy Graham died.

He was already busy saving souls
when I was born, a few months
before we dropped Fat Man and
Little Boy on Japanese civilians.

So many years since he began
the practice of calling on God
to bless people who bomb other
people. He first knelt with Nixon,

to pray before he began the secret
bombing of innocent Cambodian
civilians in the hope of gaining
advantage in a war with another

country. Later he sent Nixon
a letter urging him to bomb dikes
in Vietnam, an action that could
have led to a million, mostly
civilian, deaths. Even Nixon

wouldn't do that. Years later,
he and the first President Bush
met to pray three times the day
before Bush launched the bombing
of Iraqi troops that began the

First Iraq War. At last, traffic begins
to inch forward. I start the crawl
home through afternoon shadows.
Bombs, Billy Graham and roadwork
on the downtown connector. A lifetime.

4:00 A.M.

We know what's left. Less & less time
with miles to go to journey's end
& my mind racing no matter how I lie,
while a variant surges out of control,

with miles to go to journey's end.
The daylight we fill up is a blur,
while variants surge out of control
in a world that's asking: *what's going on?*

The daylight we fill up is a blur.
We need you, Marvin. Once again,
the world is asking: *what's going on?*
Will vaccines work on future strains?

We need you, Marvin! Once again
our worries—set free—come back to ask
whether vaccines will work on future strains?
Hopes bounce around like lotto balls.

Worries—set free—come back to ask
whether we can protect our herd
while hopes bounce around like lotto balls
& the emcee isn't laughing.

Will we be able to protect our herd?
My mind races, no matter how I lie
reminds me the emcee still isn't laughing.
But I know what's left. Less & less time.

Rainbow Connection

It's estimated that 200 species of frogs have gone extinct since the 1970s, and many fear it's a harbinger of greater biodiversity loss that will come for birds, fish, and mammals too.
   —Brian Resnick, *VOX,* December 16, 2016

My plane lifts off the runway, rises
over clogged webs of streets, highways,
flies alongside a bronze band that presses
down on Atlanta's skyline.

I turn to a crossword puzzle—1 across,
six boxes, "famous frog."

My father & I fished at night, baiting
hooks by flashlight, our lines dropped
into a white-hot orb formed by our lantern.
We didn't talk much. We never did.
We listened to crickets, waves lapping
against pilings, bullfrogs croaking.

When Erin was three, she liked to watch
Sesame Street and run through the house
shouting *Riiiiiiibbit, Riiiiiiibbit, Riiiiiiibbit*
while I laughed.

Yesterday, at the splash pad in the park
down the street, I watched screaming
toddlers bounce birdie hops in prisms
formed by the mist. At the spray's edge,
under a shrub—a forgotten plastic frog.

I write "Kermit", want space to add,
"who is dying".

Kayaking the Rio Grande

*The belief that man can control nature is
basically a twentieth century phenomenon.*
                    —National Public Radio

Banks are full, water is clean
in this timeless high desert gash
near the river's source. My paddle
blade bites deep, grabbing like a hand.
Left pull, right pull, an age-old
rhythm of work, repeated over and over,
handed down from an ancient people.

Farther south, the river sleeps,
waits for mountain snowpack
to melt, give a push for the journey
down past cities, farms, highways—
oblivious to intruders who line
its banks, steal the valley it created
—until, choking on chemicals,
it finally reaches the ocean.

I squeeze my kayak between rocks
into a racing channel. The river
washes over my body, drops me
into a pristine pool—not yet spoiled.

Houses

               we
          build our
      homes with brick,
    mud, grass. Tudor mansions
   hidden behind walls, out of sight.
 In our cities, we stack them like pallets
that stand along streets between canyon walls.
  We put locks   on the door to feel safe.
  In older days,   Druids slept in front of
 open fires, studied stars, saw magic in oaks,
mistletoe. But we clasp walls tight to roofs, hide
the sky. Windows slake our need to touch a tree.

Trees

Upright skeletons stand and testify their
resilience. The white oak king of the canopy
—upper body a tangle of naked limbs—
leans into the mountain's incline. An S
shaped adolescent poplar—each bend
marking a closed door—blazes its own
twisting trail toward sunlight. The too-
many saplings gathered underneath
wait, nervous over the start of their first
spring struggle to find space to survive.

In a few weeks, these unclothed winter
trees will begin the rebirth of the forest.
Trunks will push roots deeper in search
of stored water. Hardened buds will soften.
Thin new leaves—transparent as skin—
will emerge, thicken and darken. Leaves
will accept their role—reach out
and together weave a blanket to absorb
sun rays, catch and hold raindrops
needed for the work of master chemists.

Breath

for Clarence Clemons
(1942—2011)

How big was the Big Man? Too big to die.
Clarence doesn't leave the E Street Band
when he dies. He leaves when we die.
>   from Bruce Springsteen's eulogy
>   as reported in *Rolling Stone,* June 29, 2011

As the day's last sun pauses on the peak
of Taos Mountain, turns the snowpack
into a dazzling bulb, I watch my breath
float like gray ghosts into the chill.

For most of us, the most selfish,
thoughtless thing we do. But not for you.
You turned your breath into art. With
your saxophone, you lifted tired spirits,
made feet want to dance, made others
in the band believe they could be bigger
than they were, and they were.

Another moment, the sun drops below
the horizon on the high desert mesa.
My breath no longer visible.

Brotherhood

Seven times each day, silent monks
at Abbey of Gethsemane leave
their labor—planting, reaping, making
cheese & bourbon fudge—come
together for worship, prayer, bread, wine
& singing psalms. It's been the same,
since 1848, season after season, until
they rest on a hill of white crosses.

A few miles away, it's Bike Night
at a bar where men in leather
from Winchester, Lexington, Richmond
—sometimes all the way from Ohio—
gather near the spot where Daniel
Boone built a fort, to drink beer,
eat burgers, listen to rock & roll
and country music, shoot pool & shoot
the bull about the freedom of the ride.

Prayers end, dusk settles among
the hills. Brown-robed brothers walk
single file from the prayer room,
return to silent sanctuary behind
their "four walls of freedom."

On the gravel lot outside the bar,
helmets slide over bandanaed heads.
Hands are shaken, backs slapped.
Harleys roar to life, head down
Route 418, leaning through curves.

That Day – Sandy

*for Sandra Eileen McConnell
(1950 – 2018)*

Down a concrete path steaming
from a passing shower, I pushed
a wheelchair carrying an old friend
—a walk through the garden of Our
Lady of Perpetual Help hospice.
Past drooping hydrangeas, wilting
roses, we stopped at the tent-like
structure, behind an old oak tree
at the bottom of the hill—a place
favored by mosquitos—designated
the smoking spot. While Sandy
smoked cigarettes from a half-empty
pack, we meandered through the years:
How did we get *so damned old?*
our favorite hiking trails, Sandy's
stories about growing up "down
the bayou," the canine and feline
friends she nourished and loved
through the decades—conversation
punctuated by pauses while staring
at the canopy of poplar leaves,
listening for thunder from the fast-
moving storm. Now, barely three
weeks later, my visits are shorter.
Sandy mostly sleeps, stuffed rabbit
tucked in her arm. When awake,
talking has become too difficult.

But that day, after the mosquitos
won, long past the time the nuns
told us to be back, she smoked
the day's last cigarette—burned
down almost to ash—held to her lips
by just the tip of a finger and the tip
of her thumb. *Hey little hippie chick,
need me to find you some tweezers?*
The sound of Sandy's giggle.

End of Summer

for Sandy

She notices the way her shadow seems
to disappear at the top of sun's arc, how Saturday
Market transitions from shiny summer greens
to somber winter squash, GA peaches to pink lady

apples. Leaves stirred by squirrels chasing plops
from falling acorns affirm the passing of equinox.
Shivers from a chilly wind do nothing that stops
the hints. Next year's calendars in the mailbox

say home stretch. Eyes mist, and start to swell
at the sight of a lone wild lily after fall's first
freeze, clinging to its stalk, bidding farewell
to summer; just a few days since its last burst

of color—neither she nor the lily knowing
it would be the season's final showing.

Part Two

*Well, I'll be damned, here comes
your ghost again.*
Joan Baez—"Diamonds and Rust"

Howdy

Stranger. Don't I know you from around here?
I thought we were tight, me and my body.

    I'm sure we were tight, me and my body.
    Hurting feet on fire now seem part of your plan,

though foot pain was never ever part of my plan.
Remember all those 20-mile runs,

    our pride after PR marathon runs.
    What about the day we hiked all the way

down Grand Canyon and back. In a way
I can see how you got tired, hanging out

    with me—never satisfied—always out
    to out-do ourselves and, yes I did miss

seeing my selfishness. But I do miss
you, Stranger. I know, we're both from around here.

Erythromelalgia

> *neurovascular disorder   high rates
> of depression   suicide   affects
> only 1.3 people per 100,000   no known
> cure   few doctors ever see it   even
> fewer   are willing to treat it*

Falcons, patrolling the sky with swoops and dives
are gone. So too, bumble bees who buzzed the tired
tangle of jasmine vines that bloomed in January
—long before the bumble bees arrived.

> *symptoms: redness, swelling, pain, pins
> and needles   mostly affects feet, hands*
>
> *triggers: temperatures above 70 degrees
> stress   exercise   flares may last
> minutes   hours   days   weeks*

Feet dangle down the side of the pool, reach deep
for cooler water to shut down fire in my feet.
All that's left at the pool: me, a lost towel, the last
whiff of sunscreen.

> *in summer: can't wear shoes   can't
> go out   only quick   early morning
> dashes to CVS   Kroger   Home Depot*
>
> *in winter: layers over short sleeves
> cotton   seldom wool   backpack to carry
> sandals   and stow   layers removed
> in heated buildings*

> *in between: a couple of weeks   in spring*
> *and fall   making believe a wayward body*
> *has come home*

A pair of mourning doves I see each day light on a rail
atop a retaining wall. A few moments, and the doves flutter
down to a feeder, immerse themselves in sunflower seeds.
A cardinal takes their place on the rail.

> *always cold   life centers around avoiding*
> *flares   little decisions like when to take*
> *out the trash   requires checking the temp*
> *on the cell phone   considering what you*
> *are wearing   whether to change   how badly*
> *your feet are already hurting?*

Redbird perches tall and regal, regales himself
with songs, preens, then darts to a limb near
the doves. They quickly depart. Dusk gathers.

> *people   don't visit people*
> *who live in   cold houses*

I'm left wondering: Where do they all go?
Do the bumble bees ever want to ask me
where the blossoms went? Do the birds ever
notice their admirer? Imagine details of my
life, the way I do theirs?

> *isolation   melancholy   loneliness*

The cardinal hops to the feeder, snatches a few
fast bites, flies away.

Earth Day – 2020

A basket of caladiums catch sun's
first rays, wave toward my window,
calling me, coffee in hand, to still-cool air,
greening grass, new flowers & old
trees outside my condominium.
Aimlessly, I walk around the grounds.

Small hints tell me I'm not alone.
The perpetually preening cardinal
I consider a friend, sees me (maybe),
hops around in place like a Celtic
clogger. My neighbor barely nods
to my masked face, hurries toward
the gate where Uber drivers wait.

Otherwise, it could be another time
—a wilderness trail with a choir
of invisible birds announcing dawn;
beginning a day hike down a canyon
wall—ways I've spent other Earth Days.
But it isn't.

A few short minutes (1609 steps) & I
round the corner where my neighbor
who plants roses, lives. Then, I'm back
at my front door that opens to a chair
where I'll elevate my feet—red, swollen
& hurting—call it another day.

A Ten - Dollar Bill

Checkout line at CVS takes its time
while I study a beat-up $10 bill—faded
like old blue jeans, one corner torn off,
another permanently bent, nicked
on its side, a scar where countless folds
by countless hands almost slices Alexander
Hamilton's face from his head. I imagine

details of its life—joy the day it paid
for a rose, bought from the man in baggy
khakis who sits outside the Post Office
with flowers and a sign that reads
"Gynecologist in Training;" satisfaction,
helping to cover after-work beers
at Manual's Tavern; embarrassment,
when dropped in the collection
plate by a sinner seeking absolution
on the cheap; sadness over the kid who
bought a hit of meth before wrapping
his car around a telephone pole.

I finally reach the end of the line. The
cashier scans my box of Alocane
Emergency Gel, 4% Lidocaine, takes
my bill, turns it over and over. *Umm,
been around the block a few times, huh?*
Yep.

Rushing Down Fifty-Seventh Street

Granite wall, splotched like the back of an old
hand, I almost didn't recognize a door I once knew.
Has it been ten years? The last time she called,
she said she was finally in love. No mention
of years spent chasing a career up and down
the east coast. I push the door. It opens to a foyer
—memories of Sunday morning, fresh bagels,
hazelnut coffee—a row of mailboxes, a single
name below 4-A on paper aged to musty ocher.
I step back out, re-join the eddy of people,
carrying briefcases, tired faces, walking fast.

The Day a Love Affair Ended

Electric bulbs spread circles of light.
The gazebo in the center of the lake
disappears. Earlier, the park teemed
with people, now it seems strangely
empty: a couple of joggers, a man
walking a dog that pulls at its leash
as they move into the coming night.

And another day in the park appears
—ground freckled by sun filtered
through leaves, a grinder and monkey
dressed in matching red vests. The man
turns the crank, the monkey dances—
spinning in circles, feet appearing
to strike only air—dust clouds rise
from the leash, drug through the dirt.

Naked

Unclothed, in an examining room,
sheet hanging across my shoulders,
I examine my scars, each a mark
of past pain. My oldest scar, hidden
from all but the most intimate lovers.
Splotchy patches on my arm, almost
erased by time, a spot on my chest—
transparent as plastic, that turns red
in the sun—reminders of the day
my mother turned her back for a moment,
when I grabbed the handle of a pot
of boiling water and almost died
—a toddler's accident while learning
to climb, a young mother learning
to live, tortured by guilt. The thin,
pale path from a surgeon's scalpel,
made to repair my foot, crushed
by pieces of floorboard in a wrecked
car, a line turned wavy by shifting skin,
where a laser cut out squamous cells,
a jagged mark beside my eye left
by an elbow thrown in a playground
football game. Those others—tucked
in the corner of a secret closet—the ones
we gave each other with our tongues.

Sunrise

> *Nature, Michael, that's your church.*
> *And that's all right.*
>   Juanita Jones Abernathy, life-long
>   civil rights activist, devout Christian,
>   and my friend.

A choir assembles on rooftops, walls,
branches and wires. Darkness retreats
like chocolate melting on the tongue.
A lone congregant takes a seat, waits
in a folding chair next to the mailbox.

The first slices of sunlight creep
through space between corners,
working their way toward the spot
where the crepe myrtle waits
like a bride dressed in full bloom.

Accompanied by the choir, a homily
spoken without words, offered
by a voice within. Sunlight strikes
the crepe myrtle. It dazzles in a burst
of scarlet.
      Hosanna.

Birthday #76

picking up sticks like I did as a kid
under the pecan tree. Young squirrels spiraling

      up & down the trunk. My mind spiraling,
      shaking off the pains of aging. Leaves

shaken off, tumble to the ground, leaves
pecans hidden in piles. The squirrels scratch around

      for easy pecans, while I scratch around
      for an easy plan. Kid squirrel climbs a rooftop,

pauses a moment, leaps from the rooftop,
beckoned, no doubt, by that flaming maple.

      The kid, beckoned by that flaming maple,
      grabs a skinny limb & has to scramble.

Under the pecan tree, I still scramble
picking up sticks, like I did as a kid.

Part Three

We're suffering the result of climate change and the nuclear legacy; and we had nothing to do with either.

Tony deBrum, former Foreign Minister for The Republic of the Marshall Islands. Quoted in the —*Washington Post,* August 24, 2017

Broken Promises

The one-sided relationship between the world's most powerful nation and the Republic of the Marshall Islands, one of its most vulnerable, began near the end of World War II when U.S. troops defeated occupying Japanese forces and took control over the entire chain of islands. That relationship has proven to be a modern example of classic imperialism marked by shameless bad faith and unkept promises on the part of the U.S.

In 1947, at the U.S.'s request, the U.N. designated the Marshall Islands as a Strategic Trust Territory with the U.S as the sole trustee. Under the terms of the trust agreement, the U.S. was obligated to *promote the economic advancement and self-sufficiency of the inhabitants, and to this end . . . protect the inhabitants against the loss of their lands or resources.** Instead of adhering to that mandate, the U.S. appropriated the land and seas of the inhabitants for use as sites for 67 nuclear or thermonuclear bomb tests; left radiation so toxic it rendered some islands uninhabitable and caused birth defects and early deaths from cancer; and failed to provide adequate food, housing or medical services promised to dislocated people, a dereliction of its duty as trustee that also caused health problems and early deaths for many people. **

Besides dealing with the consequences from its islands and waters being used as nuclear weapons testing sites, the Marshall Islands is simultaneously struggling with the reality that its future existence is literally being washed away by climate change. It is one of several low-lying island nations scientists believe will become uninhabitable before the end of this century. As the single largest greenhouse gas emitter on the planet, the U.S. carries special blame and responsibility for both of the existential crises facing the Marshallese people.

It is my wish that these poems might shine some light on the faces of the Bikini people who witnessed, suffered and continue to suffer consequences from decades of duplicitous and reprehensible conduct by my country.

- See, Notes.
** See, Notes.

Bikini Atoll

located in the Republic
of the Marshall Islands

string of pearls   23 dots   middle
of Pacific Ocean   strung around 229.4
square mile lagoon   each dot

so small   total land mass   only
2 square miles   highest
elevation   7 feet   above water
at low tide

between 1946 and 1953   site of 23
nuclear   and   thermonuclear
weapons
tests

soil and water
too toxic
for human habitation
because of radiation

name
stolen
by a bathing suit

future existence
washing away
in rising seas

inhabited   3000 years ago   permanent
population today

zero

Jolet Jen Anij

I

1000 B.C.: Settlers from Southeast
Asia migrate to isolated Pacific islands
astraddle the equator. They call their
new home Jolet Jen Anij—words that
mean "Gifts from God."

1529: Spanish explorer Alvaro
de Saavedra claims Jolet Jen Anij
for Spain.

1788: An Englishman, John Marshall,
changes the name of Jolet Jen Anij
to the "Marshall Islands."

II

Ever present: The sea. The heat.
Jolet Jen Anij moves to the rhythm
of waves—breaking on the shore,
receding with its ebb. The first
sound heard upon waking,
the last before sleep.

Because of the heat, both men
and women, bare their upper bodies.
Like the seabirds, children run naked
on the beach

To feed themselves, they catch shad
in the lagoon, plant and tend taro,
and gather papayas, coconuts, breadfruit,
bananas from their bountiful trees and plants.

They make canoes from the trunks
of palm trees. From the fronds,
they make homes—to sleep
and stay safe when storms
come— and skirts that both
women and men wear,
and sails to catch the wind that
pushes their proas across the water.

Guided by maps in the night sky
and wave patterns they feel with
their stomachs, skilled seamen
sail to distant islands in proas.

The people leaving on Jolet Jen Anij
are protected by Iageach and other gods,
old as time, who live among the stars.

For as long as the oldest elders can
remember, this is how it has been.

III

Early 1800's: Germany purchases
the Marshall Islands from Spain.

1819: American missionaries arrive.

IV

One day, men whose skin has no
color and who cover their bodies
with cloth, arrive on a big ship
larger than any proa. These strange
men offer cloth and food in exchange
for coconut seeds. Then they leave.
But they keep coming back—always
wanting more seeds. They bring

missionaries who tell the people
about Jesus, who say that if the people
worship the white men's god, they
will go to a place called heaven
when they die. But the women must
cover their breasts, else they will go
to hell and burn forever when they die.

People begin to worship the white
men's god. They build a church.
Women start covering their breasts.
Mothers make children wear clothes.
They forget their old gods.

One Sunday – After Church, February 1946

I

Everyone was there to hear what
Governor / Commodore Ben Wyatt
—the man the U.S. Navy appointed
Governor—had to say. Governor
Wyatt came decked out in dress
Navy blues, a salad bar of ribbons
on his chest. He spoke from the pulpit.

He began by telling his audience
nuclear weapons were good
because they would bring peace
to the world. He told the entire
population of Bikini they were
*chosen people, like the children
of Israel.* They were told they
should agree to move to a nearby
island so the U.S. could test
new atomic weapons at Bikini.
The Governor said if they agreed
to leave, it would be *for the good
of mankind* and would *end all
world wars.* To seal the deal,
he promised they could go back
home after testing was finished,
that the Navy would help them
build houses and a church at their
temporary home, and would
provide them food until they
were able to grow their own.

The people's leader, Chief Juda,
also spoke. He told them they
*should go, everything is in God's
hand.* The people voted to leave.

A few weeks later, carrying every
thing they owned and thatching
from their church to build a new
church, every resident of Bikini
Atoll boarded a Navy ship bound
for their new home. Most chose
Rongerik Atoll, even though
elders who knew the old stories
warned that demon sisters
from Ujae often visited Rongerik.

II

Rongerik Atoll   insufficient fresh
water   poor soil   poor fishing
conditions   malnutrition
everybody sick

too close to Bikini   radioactive
fallout   fell on them   after two years
they were relocated to Kili Island

III

Kili Island   one-third of a square
mile   today   1,000 refugees still
remain there   subsisting on
imported food supplied   from trust
funds   administered   by the U.S.
high rates of diabetes   and other
obesity-related medical conditions
Spam   considered a delicacy *

IV

Return to the Promised Land

1972: Like the children of Israel,
approximately 100 Bikini evacuees
left Kili Island; returned to their
homeland, built houses, a church,
planted taro in the same dirt
as their fathers, gathered coconuts
from the same trees as their mothers,
swam and caught shad on the reef
in their ancestral lagoon.

Soon strange things began
happening. Many women had
miscarriages. The fish made
everyone sick. Everybody felt
tired.   Always. . . .

Doctors, scientists came to study
them, stuck their arms with needles,
took their blood, collected their
urine in cups, studied their blood
and urine with microscopes, cut
open coconuts and fish, looked
inside, tested the dirt, the drinking
water. They found radiation—
the silent thief who stole
their babies, robbed them of their
health—in the water they drank,
the food they ate, the lagoon they
swam and fished in, the dirt
they walked on, inside their bodies.

Navy ships took them back to Kili.

- See Notes.

Operation Crossroads – July 1, 1946, First Nuclear Bomb Test at Bikini

waves lap   gentle on the beach
in the lagoon   a single empty ship   lies
at anchor   monotonous drone   of approaching
airplane   heard   by no one

from a B-29
named
Big Stink
a bomb
named
Gilda
Rita Hayworth
painted
on its side
detonates
at 580 feet
misses
target
decommissioned
USS Nevada

July 5, 1946:   Paris swimming pool   exotic
dancer   Micheline Bernardini   introduces new
bathing suit to the world   Louis Reard   automobile
engineer / fashion designer   called his creation
"Bikini"   because he said: *like the atom bomb,*
the Bikini is small and devastating . . . .

Castle Bravo – March 1, 1954, World's First Thermo-Nuclear Bomb Test

> *6 megatons   expected yield   actual yield 14.8 megatons   1,000 times as powerful as bombs   dropped on Hiroshima and Nagasaki*

Dawn turns to daylight on Likiep Atoll,
280 miles from Bikini. An old man casts
nets into the shallows off the reef
like almost every day since his childhood.
Grandson—Tony—watches. Knowledge
passes from generation to generation.

A silent flash, brighter than the sun,
erupts on the horizon. *A bleeding ball . . .
as if you were standing under a glass
bowl, and someone poured blood over
it. Everything turned red—the ocean,
the fish, the sky. A* shock wave courses
through their bodies. Then a terrible blast
of wind. *A memory that can never
be erased.* *

> *coral rips from moorings pulverized   in an instant flung into the atmosphere radiation   floats for days falls like snowflakes*

circles the earth   pollutes
7,000 square miles of ocean
leaves a crater   6510
feet wide   50 feet deep
visible from outer space

125 miles from the blast, children
who have never seen snow, play
in the "snow" that covers the ground
on Rongelap Atoll. They eat
the "snow." Their skin turns red,
burns. They vomit.

Admiral Lewis Strauss announces
to the world: *All 230 natives appear
to me to be well and happy.*

A statement from the Navy medical
team: *We anticipate no illness.*

For decades, like human guinea pigs,
scientists will study the children
to learn long term effects from radiation
exposure. The children will learn
new words like "thyroid cancer,"
"radiation contamination," "genetic
birth defects."

- See Notes.

One Day in August – 1960

Itsy Bitsy, Tiny Weenie,
Yellow Polka Dot Bikini'
sung by teenager Bryan Hyland,
hits #1 in the U. S.
#1 in New Zealand
#8 in the U.K.

sales of Bikini bathing suits
spiking world-wide *

at Kili Island
displaced Bikini Islanders
sit down
to another dinner
of Spam

on Bikini Atoll
leftover
radioactive isotope
cesium 137
collects
in the ground

- See Notes.

The Last Remaining Eden *

Bikini Atoll

radiation level
too high
for human habitation

a few caretakers   rotate in   and out
scientists come   short visits   collect data
   go back home   write papers

divers   come on tour boats   park
offshore   a few days   lured
to lagoon   by ads
that promise

an island paradise

without a doubt the top wreck
diving destination on the planet . . .

known for its wonderful WW II
warship wreck diving

adventure divers   slide into warm
tropical water   dive deep   explore
empty rooms   on ghost ships
sunk to test

nuclear

bombs

*   See Notes

King Tides

*We are going to go under. The water is
going to keep on coming up and we're
going to have nowhere else to go.* *
—Lani Kramer, resident of Majuro, capitol
of the Republic of the Marshall Islands,
quoted in The Guardian, September 6, 2016

Far to the south, an Antarctic iceberg
calves, meanders north to warmer water
and disappears. In the Marshall Islands,
beaches creep up a little higher.

"Super moon," luminous, radiating
at its edges, hangs in the sky above
the lagoon. Each flow rises to a border
where moist gray turns white, licks
away a bit of dry dirt and swallows it.
As high tide approaches, restless water
spreads through the streets of Majuro.
Curious, but patient, it searches out
secret places, climbs the sides of Runit
Dome, concrete tomb for tons of toxic
radioactive gumbo, its cracked sides
leaking poison into the ocean.

- See Notes.

Pantoum for Junior

*In 1986, native Marshall Islander, John
Moody, moved to Springdale, Arkansas.
He got a job at Tyson Foods poultry plant
and began talking up the "land of opportunity"
in letters back home. Today, the Marshallese
community in and around Springdale
is the largest anywhere in the world other
than in Majuro. Many of them work
in local poultry processing plants.* *

August, Arkansas air, hot and heavy like home,
runs liquid down the side of a cold PBR can.
Everybody else at work, Junior's on the porch,
out on Workers' Comp.

Like liquid running down a cold PBR can,
it's always cold on the cut-up line,
but Junior's out on Workers' Comp,
not on the line of ice-chilled chickens.

It was always cold on the cut-up line.
Shoulder to shoulder with Filipe and Jamal
facing a never-ending line of iced chickens.
Reach. Grab. Slice. Drop.

Shoulder to shoulder with Filipe and Jamal,
knives slashing through the air,
Reach. Grab. Slice. Drop.
Another hour until bathroom break.

Knives slashing through the air,
about to piss in his pants,
another hour until bathroom break.
Can't fall behind. Can't reach too far.

About to piss in his pants,
no relief anywhere in sight.
Can't fall behind. Can't reach too far.
Tired, cramped shoulders aching.

No relief anywhere in sight.
Numb fingers slicing drumsticks.
Tired, cramped shoulders aching
then his blood was on the line.

Numb fingers slicing drumsticks
but Junior's home on the porch.
Today, it's another's blood on the line.
August, Arkansas air's hot and heavy, like home.

- See Notes.

Island Boy

for Tony deBrum
(February 26, 1945 – August 22, 2017)

When you were nine years old,
you witnessed the *bleeding red ball*
named Castle Bravo that scattered
radioactive fallout over the land,
the ocean, brought lifetimes
of misery, sickness, early deaths
to so many of your people.

You never forgot. That day you found
your life's work. One of the first
Marshallese people to study abroad,
you learned psychology, linguistics
and international relations at University
of Hawaii. Then you came home,
devoted yourself and talents to your
country and its people—co-author
of the Marshallese—English Dictionary,
member of the team that negotiated
the independence treaty, a diplomat,
legislator and Foreign Minister.

Like your ancient forefathers
who travelled the Pacific in proas,
you were a gifted navigator of the world
of international diplomacy—not only
by representing your country, but as
an advocate for all the people whose
land, culture and very existence is
being assaulted by the twin threats
of nuclear bombs and climate change.

You were a gentle man who mastered
the art of questioning the status-quo
with soft-spoken words. Over
and over, you challenged the world
with one simple question: *How can
the countries that create these problems
allow us to suffer.* *

Your speeches and pen carried the stories
of the world's have-nots to the halls
of international tribunals and streets
around the planet and gave the world
hope in the middle of despair.

At the 2015 Paris Climate Conference,
you united and led a coalition of over
100 developing countries. This coalition,
first confronted, then worked with leaders
from developed countries to achieve
something that had never been done.
As a leader of the most vulnerable
countries on the planet, you were instrumental
in bridging the rich/poor divide that lead
to the creation a plan, the Paris Climate
Agreement, signed by every country
in the world, that sets a goal of holding
global warming to 1.5 degrees centigrade
—a plan scientists believe can assure
 the continuation of a habitable planet.

Thank you, Tony deBrum and May
You Rest in Peace.

- See Notes.

Part Four

[L]ies, by their very nature, have to be changed, and a lying government has constantly to rewrite its own history.
—Hannah Arendt, *The Origins of Totalitarianism*

In America – November 2016

for Sally

Despite chilly fall air, a trickster sun
warmed our backs to a comfortable
sweat, hiking to the top of Blood
Mountain. Barren rock at the summit,
overlooked a line of peaks, jagged
like a saw blade. Dark shadows thrown
by fast-moving clouds slid across
unbroken forest. But the clouds were
aways off, so we took our time going
back down, not noticing them gathering.

Rocks turned slick. Wind-slung rain
stung different sides of our faces
at each switchback. We found refuge
under a granite ledge and waited—
bad weather inches away. When
fury finally turned to a steady drizzle,
we stepped out, started a slow slog
down a muddy path . . . .

In Szentendre

[A]lthough Hungary is a small country, it is one
whose creeping authoritarianism is widely admired.
   —Anne Applebaum, "Creeping Authoritarianism has Finally Prevailed"
    The Atlantic, April 3, 2020

1990: Its past marked by a history
of monarchy, totalitarianism,
alliances with Nazi-Germany
& Soviet Russia, Hungary holds
its first democratic election.

1994: A brisk business in this
holiday town of artists & galleries.
In a sun-drenched courtyard:
potted palm trees, Evian umbrellas,
strange voices, thick with palinka,
old-time rock & roll blasting through
the serving window from a boombox
in the kitchen—& me, wondering
if I was the only person there
who could understand the lyrics.

2021: A worried world watches
Hungarian democracy teetering:
anti-Semitism on the march,
Orban's neo-fascist fist pummeling
the news media—& Parliament, using
covid for cover—voting to give
Orban a green light to rule by decree.

This is what I most remember
from that day in 1994: a small
gray bird flitting around the courtyard,
landing on my table & hopping
so close I could feel the chill
from its wings on my hand. That
& Bob Seger, singing *reminisce
about those days of old* . . . .

Charlottesville

They came to Charlottesville in the summer.
They came to "Unite the Right."
They came flaunting swastikas, Nazi salutes.
They came carrying the battle flag of a lost rebellion.
They came in white hoods.
They came in camo.
They came dressed like you and me.
They came with signs.
They came with assault weapons.
They came with semi-automatic handguns.
They came in a Dodge Charger.
They left Heather Heyer dead, 19 injured.

They came with messages: *blood and soil*
    Jews will not replace us   Heil Trump
    the south will rise again   take our
    country back   white lives matter
    we will be back

Miquel

Each day, he sits with his thoughts, waiting in a cell,
replaying why they left home, the way they made
plans to find asylum. Instead, he found a jail.

He had a good life, tending coffee plants when rains fell.
But the work dried up when droughts came & stayed.
Now each day, he sits with his thoughts, waiting in a cell,

remembering the gangster who came to their home,
told Ana her brother was shot dead; being so afraid,
they left to find asylum. Instead, he found a jail.

Crossing the river, their daughter, Isabella, fell,
he carried her through water too deep for her to wade.
Now she's in detention, while he sits waiting in a cell.

The shouts: *Detener! Detener!,* Ana's screams: *Miquel,
Miquel;* the spotlights; his hopes all starting to fade.
Why do they keep them apart? Why put him in a jail?

Asylum hearings, require a lawyer to prevail,
but their savings are gone, and lawyers must be paid.
He doesn't rue a plan that went wrong, waiting in a cell.
He came seeking asylum. Instead, we put him in a jail.

Two Little Girls

for Fiona

My granddaughter, Fiona, wakes from a nap,
sees me, instead of her mother, cries over
and over, *Mommy, Mommy, Daddy, Daddy.*
I pick her up, hug her, kiss her, sing to her—
"My Girl"—while we dance around the room.
Fiona laughs.

Somewhere in South Texas, Isabella wakes
in a child detention center for migrant detainees,
sees a lady she doesn't know, cries, over and
over, *Mama, Mama, Papi, Papi.* The lady hands
her a teddy bear, hurries to another crying child.
Isabella cries.

The News

*The moment we no longer have a
free press, anything can happen.*
—Hannah Arendt, *The Origins of Totalitarianism*

Over & over on TV. Clips of Trump shouting:
The media is the enemy of the people. Crowd
chants: *CNN sucks! Lock them up! Lock them up!*

> *Across the courtyard, a woman
> prunes her roses, stops to chat with
> a neighbor. On the street, masked
> dog walkers, passing from opposite
> sides of the sidewalk, nod hellos.*

73 million people watched the first Biden / Trump
debate on TV. Trump refused to commit to peaceful
transition if he lost; told the Proud Boys, a violent,
well-known white supremacist group, *to stand
back and stand by.*

> *Voices float through acrid whiffs
> of grilling steaks & brewing coffee.
> A half-empty bottle of wine clinks
> against a glass rim. Breezes play
> irregular rhythms on wind chimes*

Trump was all-over daily news, refusing to accept
that he lost, telling the media he was considering
running again in 2024.

> *A man stands beneath a century-old
> oak tree, waters a bed of red, white
> & blue impatiens.*

Media was saturated with stories about 60+ lawsuits
filed by Trump & his allies alleging fraud. All dismissed
(some by Trump-appointed judges) because none
of Trump's lawyers could present any evidence of fraud.

> *Father & son volley on the tennis*
> *courts in the park. Sisters, dribble,*
> *take goal kicks to their mom*
> *on the soccer field.*

Tapes of Trump begging Georgia officials to change
election results played constantly on TV for weeks.

> *An Amazon driver parks her truck,*
> *drops off a package at the front door*
> *of a man who waits expectantly inside.*

January 6, 2021. Live TV: Trump tells supporters:
*if Mike Pence does the right thing, we win; walk
down to the capitol, show strength, fight like hell.*
The entire world watches a mob—some armed—
storm the Capitol, kill a police officer, injure over
100 others, search for Nancy Pelosi & Mike Pence
to assassinate them. Many rioters self-identify
as members of militia groups like Proud Boys,
Oath Keepers & Three Percenters who advocate
the overthrow of our government.

> *Around the corner, photographers*
> *gather on Jackson Street Bridge.*
> *As day turn to night, they snap shots*
> *of glowing slivers—sunlight sliding*
> *from sight between skyscrapers.*

Tonight's news: the same as last night & last
week: majority GOP-controlled states pass
laws making voting more difficult for minorities.
Swing state legislatures controlled by GOP
pass laws allowing the legislature to overrule
official election counts.

> *In the distance, the Amtrak Crescent*
> *sounds its whistle. Soon it will pull*
> *away from Brookwood Station, travel*
> *through the night to Washington, while*
> *the nation sleeps.*

Once I asked an acquaintance who grew up
in Nazi Germany, how so many people could
be fooled. *But, of course,* she said, *we did not
know. The state controlled the news. You don't
think they would tell us what they didn't want
us to know, do you?*

The End

Crows I've never seen, give a chorus of caws,
burst into foggy rain on this sad day.

Trump plays golf on this sad day.
4,000 times in Covid wards, eyes mist

watching a patient die. From the mist,
eerie warbles of a songbird I don't know

trill like chatter I don't want to know:
insurrection over election results,

calls for coup d'état. How many bad results
can come from Trump backed into a corner?

How might his twisted mind react in a corner?
An angry man lines up a two-foot putt,

like many times before. He misses his putt
and leaves the course to a chorus of caws.

Baking Banana Bread

for John Lewis
(1940 — 2020)

a good day to bake banana bread   three overripe bananas

John Lewis (that boy from Troy) crossed Edmund Pettus Bridge

for the last time   1 tsp salt   1000 Covid deaths a day

1 tsp cinnamon   U.S leads the world in Covid deaths   1 tsp

vanilla   highest unemployment since the Great Depression

1 tsp baking soda   Congress can't pass a relief bill

1 tbsp butter   for American workers   1 tbsp canola oil

Mary got Covid at a dentist appointment   ¾ cup walnut pieces

Trump keeps saying hydroxychloroquine cures Covid 19

pre-heat oven to 325   doctors say it won't and it's dangerous to

take   1 cup whole wheat flour   Jimmy got Covid in the

hospital   ½ cup white flour   hospitals running out of beds

½ cup white sugar   Black Lives Matter   ½ cup brown

sugar   Russia interfering in election to help Trump   grease

pan with butter   Trump criticizes mail-in voting   melt

remaining butter, mix with canola oil   claims it will cause election *fraud*   beat egg   *threatens to delay election*

mash bananas   *post office being sabotaged*   combine egg,

bananas, butter/canola oil   *to suppress the vote*   mix

flour, sugar, baking soda, salt, cinnamon   *mail delivery getting*

slower   blend with whisker   *postal workers say it's new*

work policies   add ½ cup of walnuts (save the rest for the top)

Trump admits slower mail means more rejected Democratic ballots

blend everything into bowl   *anti-racism protests in Portland*

spoon the mix into baking pan   *Trump sent federal agents to*

Portland   sprinkle walnuts on the top   *they detained, beat*

and tear-gassed peaceful protesters   turn off TV news

Trump has threatened not to step down if he loses   turn on E

Street Radio   *Bruce is singing "it ain't no sin to be glad*

you're alive"   pan's in the oven   *"gonna spit in the face*

of those badlands"   *what this country needs now*   tastes

pretty damn good   *"is some good trouble"*

Notes

"Broken Promises" * See, Niedenthal, Jack, "A Short History of the People of Bikini Atoll." http://marshall.csu.edu.au/Marshalls/html/History Varia/Bikini_History/Bikini_History.html

** See, "One Sunday-After Church, February 1946," Note

"One Sunday-After Church, February 1946" To find stunning and graphic poems about the conditions on Kili Island and health consequences from radiation and bad food provided by the U.S., I recommend reading *Iep Jaltok, Poems from a Marshallese Daughter* by Kathy Jetnil-Kijiner (University of Arizona Press, 2017).

"Castle Bravo" Description of the blast is a quote from a speech by former Minister of Foreign Affairs for the Republic of Marshall Islands, Tony deBrum, who, as a child, witnessed the Castle Bravo blast.

"One Day in August" During the 19th Century, missionaries converted most Marshall Islanders to a conservative nineteenth-century form of Protestantism that today is still the most common religious practice among Marshallese people. Other than at the Ronald Reagan Ballistic Missile Defense Base, bikini bathing suits are rarely seen on beaches in the Marshall Islands. Most women wear fast-drying polyester *muu-*

muus when swimming. Because bikinis expose shoulders and thighs, they run counter to Marshallese modesty customs. Somewhat ironically, many Marshallese people consider bikinis to be offensive.

"The Last Eden" title is a quote from an ad brochure by an adventure diving company.

"King Tides" In 1979, the Marshall Islands received their independence from American trusteeship and became the Republic of the Marshall Islands (RMI). For the first time since the sixteenth century, the islands were free from control by another country. Simultimeously with gaining independence, the newly created country entered into a treaty with the U.S. named Compact of Free Association ("COFA"). Several provisions in COFA were designed to partially compensate for health and welfare damages suffered by the Marshallese people due to the nuclear testing program. One provision gave citizens and nationals of the RMI the right to fully reside and work in the U.S. but without a pathway to citizenship. That provision expires in 2023 and to date, attempts to negotiate an extension do not seem promising. With 2023 approaching, exodus to the U.S. is increasing as people face the decision of either leaving now or having no place to go when their homeland becomes uninhabitable.

"Pantoum for Junior"   See, "King Tides," Note

"Island Boy"   In an interview a few months before his death, Tony deBrum, speaking with a credibility few other people possess, addressed the moral responsibility for the twin existential threats to his country:

We're suffering the result of climate change and the nuclear legacy and we had nothing to do with either. In either case, people have to choose to to end this world, this universe. You can either do it slowly with climate change, or you can press a button and blow it up. And, neither is justified.

Tony deBrum, quoted in *Washington Post*, August 24, 2017

"Baking Banana Bread"   Quotation in the last line: *what this country needs is some good trouble*, is a phrase frequently voiced by Representative Lewis.

About the Author

Michael Walls is a retired labor lawyer who lives in Atlanta. His poems have appeared in a variety of literary journals and magazines including *The South Carolina Review, The Midwest Quarterly, Poet Lore, Poetry East, San Pedro River Review, ISLE (Interdisciplinary Studies in Literature and Environment), South Florida Poetry Journal* and *Atlanta Review.* His chapbook, *The Blues Singer* was published by The Frank Cat Press in 2003 and his full-length collection, *Stacking Winter Wood* was published by Kelsay Books / Aldrich Press in 2017.

www.ingramcontent.com/pod-product-compliance
Lightning Source LLC
Chambersburg PA
CBHW071011160426
43193CB00012B/2002